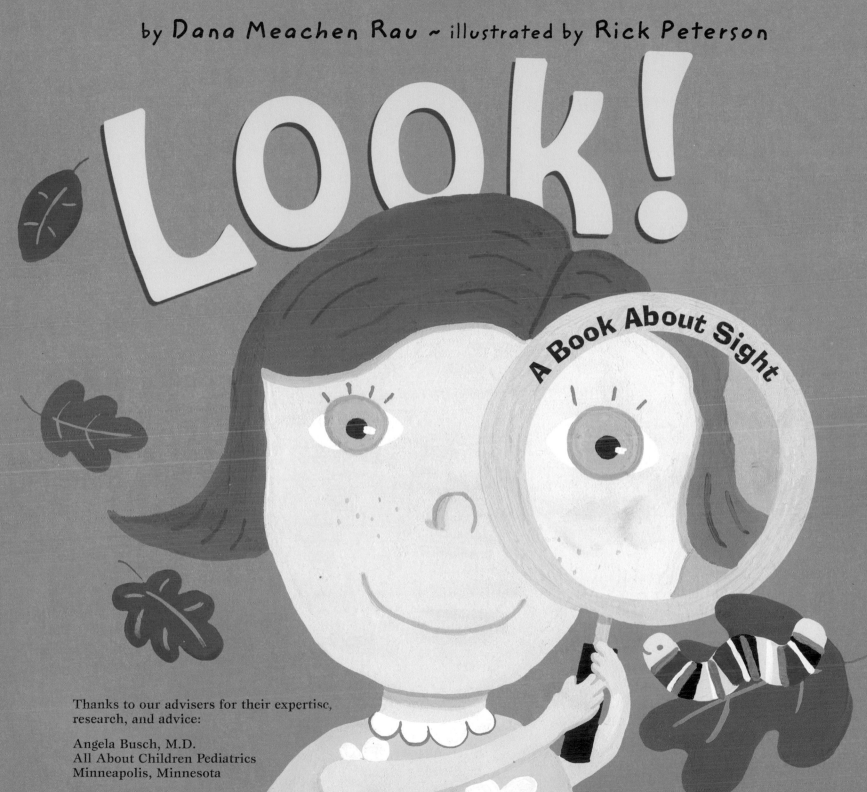

by Dana Meachen Rau ~ illustrated by Rick Peterson

LOOK!

A Book About Sight

Thanks to our advisers for their expertise, research, and advice:

Angela Busch, M.D.
All About Children Pediatrics
Minneapolis, Minnesota

Susan Kesselring, M.A.
Literacy Educator
Rosemount-Apple
Valley-Eagan (Minnesota)
School District

PICTURE WINDOW BOOKS
Minneapolis, Minnesota

Managing Editor: Catherine Neitge
Creative Director: Terri Foley
Art Director: Keith Griffin
Editor: Christianne Jones
Designer: Nathan Gassman
Page Production: Picture Window Books
The illustrations in this book are gouache paintings.

Picture Window Books
5115 Excelsior Boulevard
Suite 232
Minneapolis, MN 55416
877-845-8392
www.picturewindowbooks.com

Printed in the United States of America.

Library of Congress Cataloging-in-Publication Data
Rau, Dana Meachen, 1971-
Look! : a book about sight / by Dana Meachen Rau;
illustrated by Rick Peterson.
p. cm. — (Amazing body)
Includes bibliographical references and index.
ISBN 1-4048-1019-6 (hardcover)
1. Vision—Juvenile literature. 2. Eye—Juvenile
literature. I. Peterson, Rick. II. Title. III. Series.

QP475.7.R38 2005
612.8'4—dc22   2004019169

Look in the mirror.

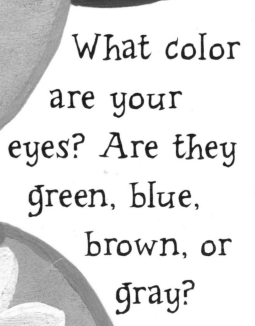

What color
are your
eyes? Are they
green, blue,
brown, or
gray?

Eyes can be many
different colors, but
their main function
is to help you see.

Your sense of sight is one of your five senses.

5

The colored part of your eye is called the iris. The black spot in the center of the colored part is actually a hole. It is called the pupil.

Your eyes are shaped like balls. They are soft and filled with a jelly-like liquid.

Your pupil changes size. It gets larger in the dark to let more light into your eye.

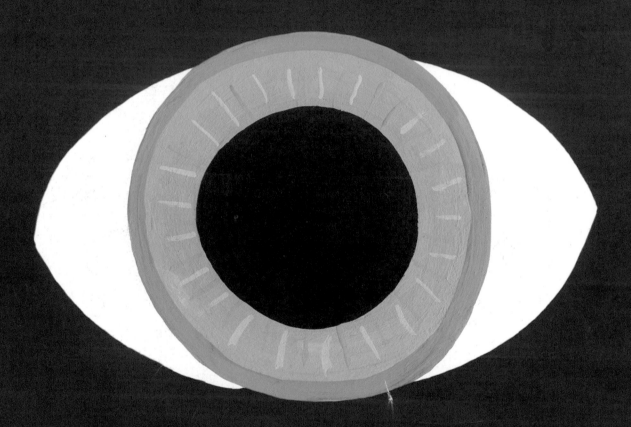

Covering your iris and pupil is a layer called the cornea. It is a clear tissue that lets light in and protects your eye.

When it is dark, it is very hard to see. That is because your eyes need a lot of light to see well.

9

You need light to see. When you look at an object, it either gives off light or reflects light. This light makes a picture of the object.

The light goes into your pupil. Then it passes through a lens. The lens makes the picture clear.

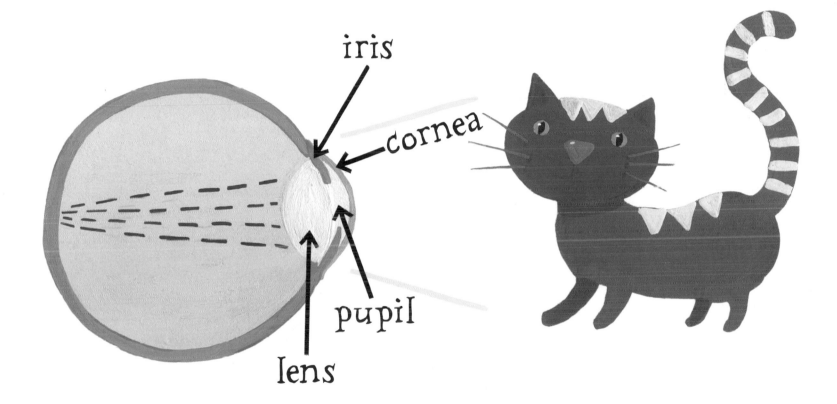

iris

cornea

pupil

lens

Some people cannot see the world clearly. They might need glasses. Glasses have lenses, just like your eyes. These extra lenses help make a clear picture for your eyes.

The picture goes to the back of your eye. This part of your eye is called the retina. Inside the retina are two types of cells called rods and cones. Rods help you see black and white. Cones help you see color.

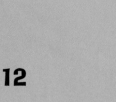

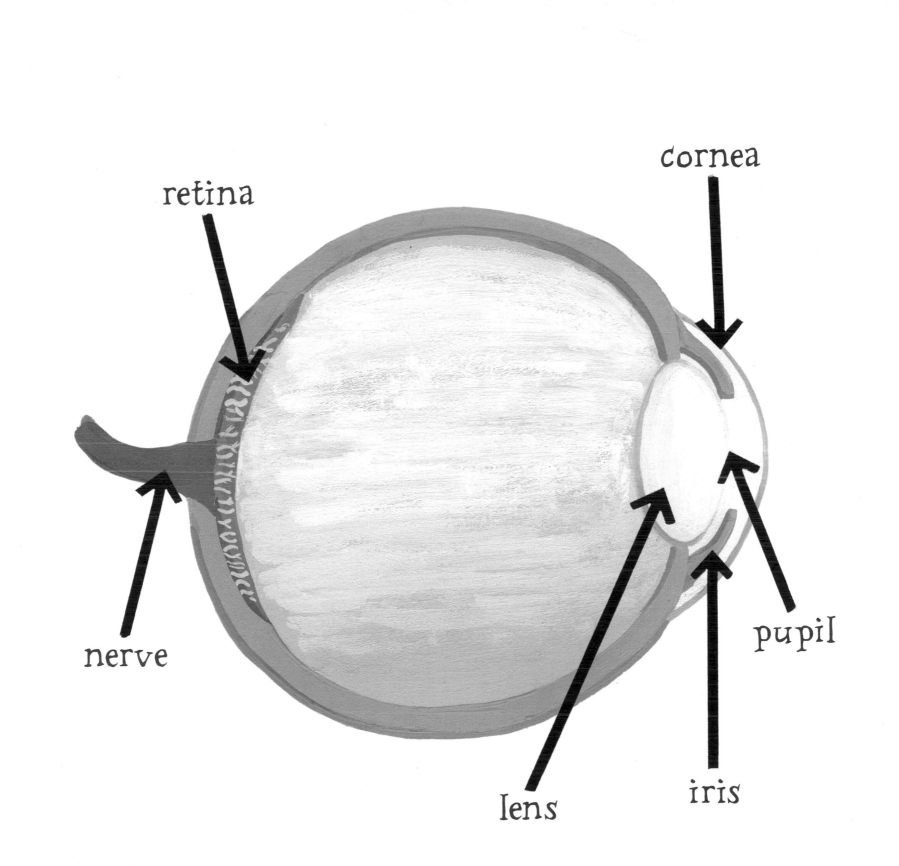

retina

cornea

nerve

lens

iris

pupil

13

Your retina is attached to a nerve. This nerve connects your eye to your brain. The nerve carries messages from your eye to your brain.

Your eyes see the shape of objects. Both a ball and a rock can be round. Your eyes know they are not the same by the tiny differences in their shapes.

Your two eyes work together to show you how far away an object is. This is called depth.

Do you ever play catch with your friends? They throw the ball to you. Your eyes focus on the ball. You can tell when the ball is getting closer to you. You are using your depth perception.

Muscles hold your eyes in place. The muscles move your eyes up and down and side to side.

Your eyes work hard and need to stay healthy. Your body has special ways to protect your eyes and keep them healthy. The thin layer of skin over each eye is an eyelid. You blink often during the day.

Look Look Look blink

Look blink Look Look

Look Look blink Look

Your eyelashes help keep dust out of your eyes. Your eyebrows help keep sweat out. If something does get in your eye, tears help wash it out.

No matter what color your eyes are, they all work the same.

Green, blue, brown, or gray eyes
all help you to see.

Eye Diagram

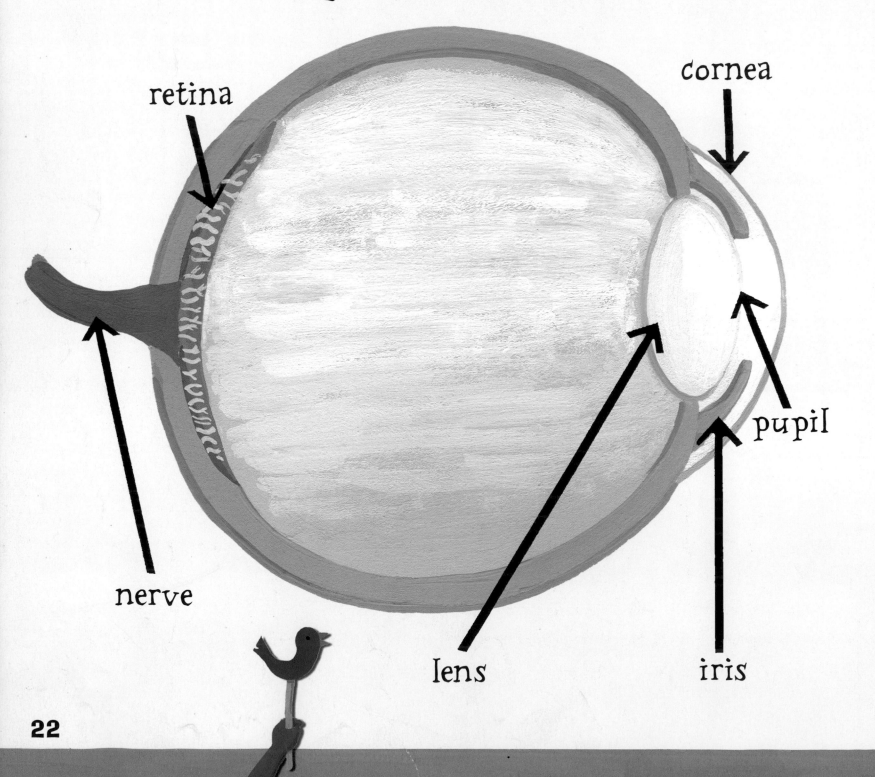

retina

cornea

nerve

lens

iris

pupil

Fun Facts

- If you are nearsighted, you can see near, but you can't see far. If you are farsighted, you can see far, but you can't see near.

- Many objects besides your eyes have lenses. Microscopes, telescopes, cameras, and glasses all have lenses.

- Most people blink every two to 10 seconds. This means your eyes are closed for about 30 minutes every day just from blinking.

Glossary

cones—the parts of your eye that see color

cornea—the clear tissue that covers the iris and pupil

depth—how near or far something is

eyelid—the thin skin over your eye

iris—the colored part of your eye

lens—the part of your eye that helps focus the picture

nerves—cords running through your body that get and give messages to your brain

pupil—the hole in the center of your iris

retina—the back part of the inside of your eye

rods—the parts of your eye that see black and white

To Learn More

At the Library

Cole, Joanna. *You Can't Smell a Flower with Your Ear! All About Your Five Senses.* New York: Grosset & Dunlap, 1994.

Hurwitz, Sue. *Sight.* New York: PowerKids Press, 1999.

Nelson, Robin. *Seeing.* Minneapolis: Lerner Publications, 2002.

On the Web

FactHound offers a safe, fun way to find Web sites related to this book. All of the sites on FactHound have been researched by our staff. www.facthound.com

1. Visit the FactHound home page.

2. Enter a search word related to this book, or type in this special code: 1404810196

3. Click on the fetch it button.

Your trusty FactHound will fetch the best sites for you!

Index

cones, 12

cornea, 8, 11, 13, 22

depth, 16, 17

eyebrows, 19

eyelashes, 19

eyelid, 18

iris, 6, 7, 8, 11, 13, 22

lens, 11, 13, 22, 23

muscles, 17

nerves, 13, 14, 22

pupil, 6, 7, 8, 11, 13, 22

retina, 12, 13, 16, 22

rods, 12

Look for all of the books in the Amazing Body series:

Bend and Stretch: Learning About Your Bones and Muscles

Breathe In, Breathe Out: Learning About Your Lungs

Gurgles and Growls: Learning About Your Stomach

Look! A Book About Sight

Look, Listen, Taste, Touch, and Smell: Learning About Your Five Senses

Shhhh… A Book About Hearing

Sniff, Sniff: A Book About Smell

Soft and Smooth, Rough and Bumpy: A Book About Touch

Think, Think, Think: Learning About Your Brain

Thump-Thump: Learning About Your Heart

Yum! A Book About Taste